EVERYDAY YOU

Create Your Day with Joy and Mindfulness

ERIC MAISEL

PHOTOGRAPHS BY DANIEL TALBOTT

Conari Press

First published in 2007 by Conari Press,
an imprint of Red Wheel/Weiser, LLC
With offices at:
500 Third Street, Suite 230
San Francisco, CA 94107
www.redwheelweiser.com

Library of Congress Cataloging-in-Publication Data available upon request

ISBN-10: 1–57324–286–1
ISBN-13: 978–1–57324–286–8

Cover and interior design by Maija Tollefson
Cover and interior photographs © Daniel Talbott

Printed in China
MD

10 9 8 7 6 5 4 3 2 1

CONTENTS

INTRODUCTION

You can create the life you want by focusing on three simple ideas: joy, mindfulness, and connection. Each of these three seems to have gotten lost in the fracture of modern life: joy falling down a rabbit hole and vanishing like the White Rabbit; mindfulness replaced by to-do lists, television commercials, and mental chatter; and connection transformed into Internet surfing and families with more cell phones than conversations. These are great losses.

In these pages I invite you to remember some simple things: that joy is available and that joy matters; that mindfulness is available and that mindfulness matters; that connections are available and that connections matter. Your heart warmed, your mind quieted, your arms outstretched: is there really a better philosophy of life? Take each page of this book as it comes—a few words, a small exercise, an image—in the same simple way that it is offered, as itinerant poets offer their verses on the road we all travel together.

Create your day as you might set your table, adding a bouquet of joy, a candle of mindfulness, a stunning centerpiece of connection. The work of life never goes away, whether we find ourselves in the private hours of dawn or the bright light of midday employment. But that work is made easier by a new, genuine openness to joy, thoughtfulness, and connection. Open this book and open up to your brand new day.

EVERYDAY JOYFUL 1

How will you bring new delight into your life? What pathways to joy will you explore? What follows are thirty suggestions. I invite you to embrace the idea that joy is an attitude; that wonder is a special doorway to joy; that deep joy arises out of mystery; and that friendship, play, exploration, and relaxation are each sunlit avenues on the road to joy. Let your joyous journey begin!

OBSTINACY

Decide to be joyful.
Really commit!
Feel the joy rise up within you.

Grow joyful through obstinacy.

Make a fist. Shake it. Shout, "I will be
joyful!" Chuckle at your little display of
obstinacy but treat the idea seriously. A
stubborn commitment to joy is necessary
for joy to take hold.

ATTITUDE

Joy is an attitude.
A decision to side with life.
A conscious, loving opening.

Grow joyful by embracing joy.

When you wake up, stretch and say, "I will enjoy this day!" Try smiling rather than frowning as you get ready for work. Let joy circulate with your blood supply even as your day fills up with stresses and challenges.

DREAM

Life wears us down.
Our dreams fade.
Joy marches out.

Grow joyful by dreaming again.

Create a list of beautiful dreams. Try not to censor yourself or dismiss your dreams out-of-hand. Pick a dream from your list and make it your new goal. Can you feel the joy well up in you, despite your doubts?

WONDER

It is a miracle that we don't melt in the bath.
It is amazing that termites build breezeways.
It is astounding that we get a billion second chances.

Grow joyful by opening to wonder.

What wondrous place have you been long-
ing to visit? A bakery across town, a beach
down the coast, a monthly jam session, a
specialty bookstore? Pick a place and a day
and make a joyous expedition.

LAUGHTER

There are 206 bones in the human body.
Not counting the funny bone.
Remember that one?

Grow joyful through laughter.

Rent a funny movie. Read a funny book.
Make a funny face. Embrace silliness as a
path to joy. Even science decrees that
laughter is the best medicine. Make it a
priority to laugh.

MYSTERY

Life's mysteries prompt many feelings.
Awe, surprise, even fear.
And, to the ready heart, profound joy.

Grow joyful by opening to mystery.

Get ready for the night. When it's dark out-
side, find a spot where you can see the sky.
There are no questions to pose or answers
to receive. Just let mystery course through
you like a wave.

SURRENDER

Give up your commitment to sourness.
Quiet your critical nature.
Release your bile, your anger, your
resentment.

Grow joyful through surrender.

Name a grievance that really upsets you:
the critical things your mother used to say,
the unfriendliness of a neighbor, the diffi-
culty of your commute. Breathe gently and
begin to smile. Let the grievance evaporate
like mist on a sunny morning.

ACHIEVEMENT

Work well.
Admire your efforts and your results.
Take satisfaction in a job beautifully done.

Grow joyful through accomplishment.

Select a big project whose completion
would make you proud. Create a plan for
reaching your goal and execute your plan.
Smile each day as you picture your project
completed beautifully.

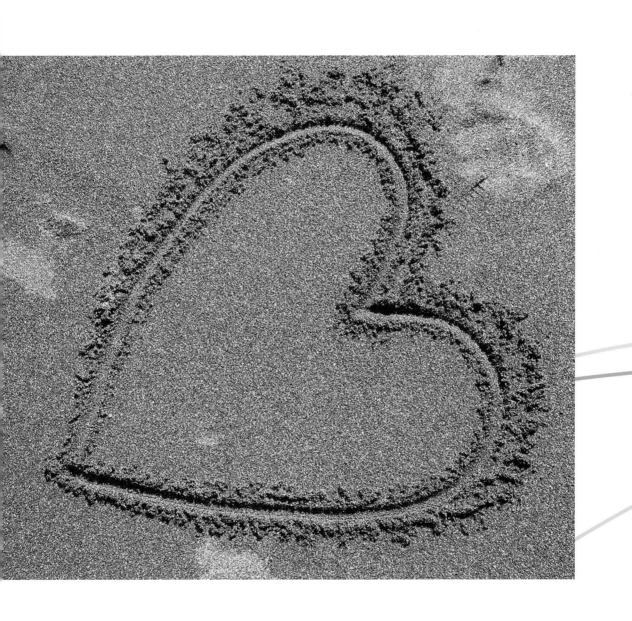

HEART

Mingled breath.
Funny habits.
A history of sorrow and happiness.

Grow joyful through intimacy.

Fall in love with your loved one again.
Open to love; bring roses; bring kisses.
Let the old hurts vanish. Promenade
down a leafy boulevard, you and your
lover hand-in-hand, doing nothing.

FREEDOM

Cut class.
Go down to the river.
Skip stones until it's time for ice cream.

Grow joyful by breaking free.

Pick an important but not vital obligation,
one that would take three or four hours to
complete. Chuck it. Do something joyful
instead—without feeling guilty!

EXPLORE

Pick a subject that fascinates you.
Get a pile of books out from the library.
Curl up on the sofa and investigate.

Grow joyful by exploring.

We avoid exploring new subjects because
we fear that there's too much to learn. Let
go of that excuse. Pick a subject—Finnish
literature, Chicago jazz, island architec-
ture—and expand your horizons!

PLAY

Pick a game you love.
Marbles, hide-and-seek, croquet.
Play it until it's too dark to see.

Grow joyful by playing.

What games did you once enjoy? Volleyball?
Scrabble? Badminton? What have you
longed to try? Trivial Pursuit? Poker? Ping
pong? Do it! Call some friends, make a date,
have some light-hearted fun.

CHAT

Make a lunch date.
See an old friend.
Laugh and giggle.

Grow joyful in conversation.

Remember Jane? How long has it been?
Drop her a line. If she's receptive, make
a lunch date. Over a long lunch, chat
for hours.

REBIRTH

Dawn breaks.
A glorious rebirth.
Repeated endlessly.

Grow joyful with the new day.

Dawn is nature's masterpiece. Get up early.
Feel the possibility in a brand new day. Hug
your coffee cup for warmth and smile as
the sun suddenly rises.

FRIENDSHIP

The fishing trip.
The shopping spree.
The easy camaraderie.

Grow joyful with friends.

Plan an uncomplicated party, nothing that requires deep housecleaning. Invite a handful of friends, set out the crackers and cheese, and enjoy the company of likeminded people.

FORGET

The arrow struck.
The pain was intense and real.
But remembering only salts the wound.

Grow joyful through forgetfulness.

Bring up a disabling memory. Once the emotion subsides, say "I will never remember this again." Trust that your psyche agrees. Allow yourself a little shiver of joyous release.

CHILDHOOD

Playgrounds, parks, schoolyards.
Remember when you ran all day?
Refresh that memory where children gather.

Grow joyful among children

When the weather is good, pack a picnic
lunch and head for the zoo. Find a spot
where you can watch the children. Spread
out your blanket and bask in their laughter.

Stretch out.
Push "Play."
Let the director whisk you
to Paris or Madrid.

Grow joyful by relaxing.

Go to the foreign movie section of a well-stocked video store. Select two or three movies. Spend all day on a cheap vacation to places where the language and the light are different.

SING

Get in the shower.
Hum or belt out an aria, a ballad, a carol.
Be the envy of angels.

Grow joyful by singing.

Listen to the songs that were playing when
you went to high school. Sing right along
with them. Become a pop star in your living
room and bring down the house.

INDULGE

You don't have to cash in your retirement account.
You don't have to get a second job.
Small pleasures are inexpensive and abundant.

Grow joyful by indulging in small pleasures.

Go to your favorite gift store. Buy that
eight-hour candle, that blue bud vase, that
journal in suede. Have it wrapped as a gift.
When you get home, exclaim, "My, who
could have bought me *this*?"

FASCINATING

The eyes of your lover.
The continents you haven't visited.
Lavender growing in a corner of your garden.

Grow joyful by opening to fascination.

Journey to a nearby haunt to explore a
lighthouse, a flea market, a rock formation,
a field of strawberries. Get started early and
spend the day blissfully fascinated.

THANKS

Give thanks for the Bill of Rights.
For deep dish pizza.
Or?

Grow joyful by giving thanks.

Write a thank-you note to someone who
deserves it, maybe to your third grade
teacher who always smiled when you raised
your hand or to the friend who waters your
plants when you're on vacation . . . Write a
heart-felt note and post it.

CREATE

You could write a gorgeous sonnet.
Maybe not at the first crack.
But eventually. And joyously.

Grow joyful by creating.

Have you been putting off some creative
project? Open up to your creative nature
and dive right in. Maybe you'll create a
masterpiece, maybe you'll make a mess.
Let the gods of whimsy decide.

INTEGRITY

Upholding your ideals is a powerful pleasure.
Manifesting your moral nature.
Acting authentically.

Grow joyful by living your principles.

Pick a cause to champion. If it's local, drive
right over. If it's global, surf the Net, join
an organization, and pledge your help.
Smile as you invest your time, your money,
your energy.

HOPE

Life grinds. Hope is lost.
But a small flame still flickers.
Turn that flame into a fire of hopefulness.

Grow joyful through renewed hope.

Pledge that you'll renew hope every day. Your affirmation might be "I have a good feeling about today," "I can't wait to see what today brings," or just "Hello, new day!"

LOVE

Love is the direction.
Love is the option.
Love is the answer to every tricky question.

Grow joyful by manifesting your loving nature.

Turn your loving feelings into loving
actions. Target someone to receive your
love. It might be your mother, your little
sister, or you. Yes, or you!

NATURE

Bark peeling.
Bare tree limbs.
Sap oozing.

Grow joyful in nature.

Do the mountains call to you? The desert?
The deep forest? Make a pilgrimage to a
spot you love. Carve out time to enjoy
yourself, to pick wildflowers and to watch
the sparrows play.

LIVE

Maybe we return as butterflies.
Maybe we return as soot.
Maybe our journey surpasses
understanding.

Grow joyful by embracing life.

Get out your calendar. Pepper next month's
boxes with joyful larks and escapades. Plan
for love, for fun, for laughter. Don't let three
days running go by without a notation.

TODAY

Today is a day to be joyful.
Rejoice!
Rejoice!

Grow joyful this very day.

What will you do today to bring joy to your
heart? Look at picture albums, make that
special dessert, love that special someone?
Why settle for just one joyous moment?
Have eleven!

EVERYDAY MINDFUL 2

You are what you think. Think carelessly and you'll trip over your untied mental shoelaces. Think aimlessly and you'll lose your way in the thick underbrush. Grow mindful and you'll make yourself proud. Silence, breath awareness, focused attention, a meditative attitude, detachment, keen observation, and structured practice are some of the keys to mindfulness. Embrace the thirty suggestions that follow and get a grip on your mind!

NOW

Live in the present moment.
Not in the past. Not in the future.
That is the essence of mindfulness.

Grow mindful by embracing now.

Mindfulness is the practice of coming to
a stop and noticing the content of your
thoughts and the richness of the present
moment. Try this now, without further ado.

YOU

What sort of practice is mindfulness?
It is the practice of ego-less concentration.
The exorcism of fear, pettiness, and narcissism.

Grow mindful by letting go.

Sit quietly. Let everything that is "you" slip away. What remains is your core, your true self. By practicing, learn how to access the deeper you behind the everyday you.

AWARE

Observe your thoughts.
Like a bird watcher in a great preserve.
Know your own mind.

Grow mindful through self-reflection.

Do you know how your mind spends its day? Choose a two- or three-hour period and get acquainted with the actual content of your thoughts.

SILENCE

Silence is the ground of mindfulness.
In silence you become aware.
Of a leaf. Of a solution. Of an intention.

Grow mindful by inviting silence.

Create a quiet spot. Dim the lights. Close
the curtains. Sit up straight. Grow very
still. Fill yourself with your own wisdom.

BREATHE

A breath is a container for consciousness.
When you notice your breathing,
you stop running.
You reclaim your faculties.

Grow mindful through breath work.

Practice taking long, deep breaths—five
seconds on the inhale, five seconds on the
exhale. Several times a day stop everything,
shut your eyes, and attend to your breathing.

MEDITATE

What is meditation?
Just a way to grow quiet.
Just a way to focus.

Grow mindful through meditation practice.

Explore formal meditation through reading,
listening to meditation tapes, taking a class,
or going on a retreat. Find a philosophy and
a style that suit you.

ATTENTION

You can rush by every sight and signpost.
You can slow down and pay attention.
Which will you choose?

Grow mindful by paying attention.

Drive ten miles an hour slower than usual.
Take in your neighborhood. Notice the
oleander growing down the median. Let
the look of the sky infiltrate your heart
and inform your understanding.

DISTRACTIONS

A thought pulls you this way.
A thought pulls you that way.
Wrest control and get a grip.

Grow mindful by eliminating distractions.

What distracts you? Worries about money?
Negative self-talk? Whenever your awareness is pulled away by a distracting thought,
tug your mind back as if it were leashed.

FLUID

Endless ocean waves.
The rhythm of the trance.
Moments like breaths.

Grow mindful through flow.

When your awareness is pure, when distractions have been eliminated, you enter a trance state known as flow. In this state creation and revelation occur. Try it!

DETACH

You are not your thoughts.
You are not your feelings.
You are a beautifully endowed observer.

Grow mindful through detachment.

Notice the next time you grow angry. If
your anger is pure reflexive indulgence
and serves no good purpose, shout "Go
away, anger! I don't need you!" Be bigger
than your thoughts and feelings.

ACTION

Mindfulness leads to right action.
You become aware of the thing to do.
Then you must do it.

Grow mindful by following through.

As you practice mindfulness you become
aware of the things that you must do.
Make a pledge to find the courage and
discipline to accomplish the tasks your
clear mind has named for you.

FOCUS

If you glance everywhere you see nothing.
Focus your field of vision.
Really look.

Grow mindful by focusing.

Go to the beach. Pick up the first seashell
you spot. Study your prize. Memorize its
ridges and whorls. Give it five minutes of
total attention.

STRUCTURE

Mindfulness is a practice.
Every practice needs structure.
What structure will you choose?

Grow mindful by imposing structure.

You might sit quietly for twenty minutes
two or three times a day. You might keep a
mindfulness journal. Or you might take a
slow walk to the same spot every morning.
Build the structure that's right for you.

OBSERVATION

Seeing is an art form.
Ask any artist.
Become an artist of the passing parade.

Grow mindful by noticing.

Find an outdoor café. Order a tall drink.
Watch the people passing. Write down
what you see: details of their clothing,
features of their faces, your hunches
about their inner life.

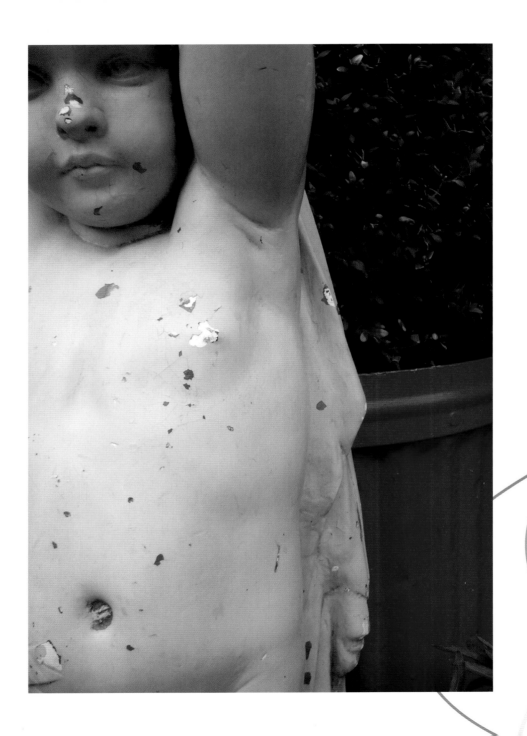

EXPERIENCE

Experience is the great teacher.
Learn life's lessons.
Let reality reform your brain.

Grow mindful by learning from experience.

Have a new experience. Take a monoprinting class, travel halfway up Everest, volunteer at a shelter. Keep a journal and every night record—better yet, make sense—of your experience.

PATIENCE

Mindfulness requires a patient attitude.
An acceptance of the rhythms of life.
A willingness to slow down and settle in.

Grow mindful by practicing patience.

What tasks do you always rush? Visits to
your parents? Eating dinner? Driving to
work? Next time be mindful and whisper,
"Patience, patience."

MOVEMENT

Engage in ritual movement.
Take control of your body.
Your mind will follow.

Grow mindful through movement.

Begin a walking meditation practice. Go to a park with a path. Walk slowly, listen to the songbirds, smell the perfume of the flowers. Think thoughts or think nothing.

STAGES

What is right thinking at age ten? At age sixty?
Different ages have their different objectives.
Mindfulness is a seasonal affair.

Grow mindful according to your stage in life.

What should you pay attention to these
days? Relationships? Career? The wider
world? Your garden? Meditate on the
question, "What is the purpose of this
moment?"

STOP

The essence of mindfulness is cessation.
No more running. No more racing.
No more scratching away at an eternal to-do list.

Grow mindful by completely stopping.

Say to your self, "I am stopping now."
Consciously release your worries and your
thoughts about your next tasks. Sit, breathe
deeply, and really stop for a few minutes.

CHATTERBOX

Your mind can become a frantic chatterbox.
Full of worries, regrets, gossip.
Hush that noise. Quiet those voices.

Grow mindful by quieting mind chatter.

Notice an unnecessary thought and
consciously let it go by saying, "Away
thought." Eliminate another. Keep going.
Eliminate so many unnecessary thoughts
that the remaining ones experience real
elbow room.

CONSIDER

We make our decisions impulsively.
Without stopping to really consider.
Mindfulness is the opposite procedure.

Grow mindful by weighing options.

Bring a current dilemma to mind.
Generate a list of possible solutions,
as many as a dozen. Examine each
option in turn, mindfully considering
its pros and cons.

REFRESH

Our thoughts grow stale.
Our opinions shopworn.
Splash some cold water on
your habits of mind.

Grow mindful by refreshing your thinking.

Place two chairs facing one another. Pick an
issue that matters to you. Move from chair
to chair articulating both sides of the issue.
Air your current thoughts and your latest
arguments. Discover what you know.

STRETCH

You could stop at the border of the known.
Many do.
But mindfulness waits across the river.

Grow mindful by stretching.

Ask yourself, "What would I love to
learn next?" Name the next step in
your education. Stride to the precipice
of the unknown and dive headlong
into "don't know."

MYSTERY

At the heart of mindfulness is mystery.
The mystery of the known.
The mystery of the unknown.

Grow mindful by embracing mystery.

Make a love of mystery part of your
practice. When you look at your buttered
toast, your tile floor, or your lover's brow,
shake your head and whisper, "How
deliciously mysterious!"

PRESSURE

Mindfulness is easier in a serene monastery.
Growing vegetables. Praying. Making brandy.
But we practice our mindfulness in bedlam.

Grow mindful under pressure.

Go to a busy place—a department store
during Christmas rush, the post office on
April 15th, Grand Central Station on any
day. Perform your mindfulness practice
in the midst of a roiling crowd.

SPEED

You have a moment between meetings.
Is that time enough to deepen your awareness?
It is if you have been practicing mindfulness.

Grow mindful at the speed of life.

Say, "I can achieve quiet awareness in the
blink of an eye. I can live mindfully even
in a hurricane." Practice until you can.

INTENTION

Intend from a deeper place than ego.
Intend from a deeper place than desire.
Intend with all of your humanity.

Grow mindful through right intention.

Make a short list of your major goals in life.
Read the list over. Memorize it. As part of
your mindfulness practice, bring this list of
prime intentions to mind every day.

CHOOSE

Mindfulness is a choice you make.
Choose to focus your awareness.
Choose to deepen your experience.

Grow mindful by choosing mindfulness.

With awareness comes a clear understanding
of our mistakes and messes. Why invite it,
then? Because that understanding liberates us
and allows us the possibility of making fewer
mistakes in the future.

RESPONSIBILITY

Mindfulness is not a tactic.
It is a tool to build character.
A light to illuminate right living.

Grow mindful by taking responsibility.

No one can assign you responsibility. You,
however, must assign it to yourself. Keep
track of the tasks and goals illuminated by
your mindfulness practice, by maintaining a
special journal devoted to that purpose.

TODAY

Maybe you spent yesterday woolly-headed.
Never mind.
Today is the perfect day for clarity and wisdom.

Grow mindful today.

Begin your practice of focused awareness
today. Enjoy a calm that only comes with
the conscious application of mind and
heart. Stop, settle yourself, and grow
aware of the truth within you.

EVERYDAY CONNECTED 3

The touch of another person's hand, a salty breeze coming in off the ocean, the sharp dialogue you create for your novel: if we are not connected to other people, to nature, to our own creative self, to our community, to our work, and to our family and friends, our heart grows cold, our thoughts turn bleak, and our mood darkens. Use the following thirty suggestions to foster new connections and begin to reap the rewards of relating!

GENERATIONS

From the dawn of time
To the present moment,
You are part of the vast
unfolding.

Grow connected through shared
human history.

You exist by virtue of an unbroken line
dating back to the dawn of our species.
Feel the beauty of that necessary connection. Set aside some time to reflect on
that poignant fact.

VALUE

Connection heals.
Connection satisfies.
Connection matters.

Grow connected by valuing connection.

Make a list of reasons to strengthen your connection with your intimates, your community, your family, your work, yourself. Take the time to make a list that impresses you and convinces you of the value of connections in your life.

HEART

Strong affection,
Strong connection.
Lead with your heart.

Grow connected through love.

Where would you like to lavish a little
more loving attention? On your child?
On your mate? On the creative work
you do? Once you decide, open your
heart in that direction.

UNIVERSAL

An energy courses through everything.
Electrical, mystical, whatever its name is.
You are made of the same stuff.

Grow connected to the universe
metaphysically.

Sit quietly. Close your eyes. Empty your
mind of its usual business. Breathe regularly
and deeply. Listen to the faraway silence. You
and the universe are indistinguishable.

WILLING

Relationship is an art.
Relationship is a practice.
But first of all relationship is a willingness.

Grow connected by choosing connection.

Write out on a sheet of paper "I am willing to make new connections." Below that write "I am eager to relate." Below that write "I mean it!" Repeat these three sentences out loud, with conviction.

SELF

Your first connection is with yourself.
You holding your hand.
You singing your praises.

Grow connected through self-relationship.

Make it a top priority to improve the way
you think about yourself, talk to yourself,
and treat yourself. Begin by saying, "I am
my own best friend and advocate!"

FRIENDSHIP

Call a friend.
Check in.
Swap some stories.

Grow connected through friendship.

Which dear friend haven't you seen in a
while? Send him or her an e-mail. As the
two of you plan your time together, open
your schedule wide and give generously
of your time.

COMMUNITY

Wherever you live
Small town, suburb, metropolis
Your community is waiting.

Grow connected by embracing community.

Is there a community project worth
your time and attention? A national issue
with a local connection? Devote a weekday
evening or a Saturday morning to
community involvement.

LABOR

We earn our bread.
When the connection is there,
It tastes more like cake.

Grow connected at work.

Ask yourself the question, "How can I feel
more connected at work?" Breathe deeply,
take your time, and meditate on the
question until useful answers emerge.

FAMILY

That odd aunt.
That prankster cousin.
Our parents, warts and all.

Grow connected with family.

Are you feuding with a family member?
Have you grown distant, even estranged?
Look into your heart and see if you want to
make an overture of friendship, a gesture
of love.

CLOSER

Take a step forward.
Then another.
Draw closer.
Then the gap vanishes.

Grow connected through intimacy.

Make a conscious effort to embrace your partner, your child, a friend—to close the gap between you, to feel closer. Do this without fanfare and do it now.

MEMORY

That swimming hole.
That picnic spot.
The feel of summer nights.

Grow connected by remembering.

Make a tall glass of iced tea. Sit outdoors in
the shade. Think back to your childhood.
Focus on the good memories, the sweet
feelings. Feel connected to your youth.

HEARTH

Blazing fire in the fireplace.
Candles on the table.
Light, warmth, comfort.

Grow connected in your own home.

Create a homey spot where you can read,
listen to music, and dream. Turn at least a
portion of your house into a real home—
and make sure to use it.

PLACE

That seashore village.
Paris, London, Rome.
The town where you were born.

Grow connected to a place you love.

Plan a trip to a place that holds meaning for you. If you can't get away, visit it vicariously through books, photos, or brochures. Feel a visceral connection to that place for at least a few hours.

EARTH

Sun blazing.
A fresh breeze up.
Your bare feet in the soil.

Grow connected to the earth.

Get out into nature. Step off the path, take
off your shoes, and walk in the grass. Get
some dirt lodged between your toes.

FESTIVE

Send out invitations.
Put on some music.
Open the door when the bell rings.

Grow connected by celebrating.

Throw an informal party. Make it large
enough that your home rings with laughter
and good cheer. Get those invitations out
before another season passes.

CREATE

That story you've been meaning to write.
That pottery class you've been meaning to take.
That music you've been meaning to play.

Grow connected with your muse.

Name a creative project you've been intending to start. Put aside your fears and doubts, get your materials together, roll up your sleeves, and jump right in.

HAPPY

A silk thread of joy
Runs through the ordinary.
Can you feel it?

Grow connected through joyfulness.

What would you enjoy doing today?
Watching a movie with a bag of popcorn?
Walking by the sea? Shopping downtown?
Name a favorite joy and indulge it.

BODY

You aren't ethereal.
You need fuel, exercise, sunlight.
Who is the guardian of your temple?

Grow connected to your body.

Don't call it a diet, call it a wackadoo.
Don't call it exercise, call it funeree.
Create a personal language that erases
memories of broken resolutions and
inspires healthy habits. Get on with
your wackadoo and funeree!

CHILDREN

Their special laughter.
Their games, their antics.
Our shared future.

Grow connected where children play.

Make a pilgrimage to a park or playground.
Open your heart to the children you see
there. Sit on a bench and prepare to smile
and chuckle.

REPAIR

A disconnection has occurred
Between you and someone you love.
How will you heal the wound?

Grow connected by making repairs.

Pick a person with whom you would like
to reconnect. Name what is needed to
repair the break: a cleansing conversation,
forgiveness, a little loving effort. Make
your repairs.

SEAMLESS

Separation is an idea.
Alienation is a concept.
Connection is an option.

Grow connected through right thinking.

Get a grip on your mind. Decide that you
would rather make connections than live
a lonely, isolated life. Argue well and
convince yourself.

NEIGHBORLY

Wave hello.
Say a few good-natured words.
Tear down a fence with a smile.

Grow connected with your neighbors.

Is there a neighbor you've been meaning
to get to know? Someone sitting at the
cubicle down the hall? The couple just the
other side of your lawn? Break out a bag of
cookies and visit.

PASSION

Do your goals make your blood race?
Are your dreams lofty ones?
Do you honor your deepest desires?

Grow connected through your passion.

Choose some new goals that you truly
desire. At the same time, invest at least a
little fiery passion in your current projects
and your present life.

NETWORK

You take a business card.
You leave a business card.
Eddies of energy are created.

Grow connected by networking.

You will achieve your goals much more
easily if you establish contacts, create
advocates, locate leads, and connect with
like-minded people. Network today and
every day.

PLAN

You feel terribly alone.
Completely disconnected.
What will you do?

Grow connected by having a plan.

Create a simple plan that you can put
into action whenever you feel isolated.
Your plan might include dinner with a
friend, a family visit, attending a class,
or volunteering your services.

LEISURE

You have a few free hours.
You could hibernate.
Or you could make a heartfelt connection.

Grow connected in your free time.

Reconnect with a hobby you once enjoyed
or investigate a new pastime. Consider what
would make for a meaningful avocation
and begin to actively pursue it.

TEAMWORK

Can you build a bridge by yourself?
Maybe—but only a small one.
Not a bridge that spans any real distance.

Grow connected through teamwork.

Do you need a team in order to accomplish
an important goal? Have you been putting
that team-building off? Sit down with a pen
and some paper and make a list of who you
want on your team.

SHARING

Make room in your psyche.
Make room in your heart.
Make room in your schedule.

Grow connected by sharing your life.

Look at your schedule for the coming
month. How much time have you set
aside for deepening connections? If it's
too little, double it, triple it, quadruple it.

TODAY

Reach out to one person.
Make one human connection.
Start a relationship.

Grow connected today.

Be mindful of your desire to connect with
people, with your job, with your community,
with all aspects of your life. Stop, reach out,
and make heartfelt connections right now.

TO OUR READERS

Conari Press, an imprint of Red Wheel/Weiser, publishes books on topics ranging from spirituality, personal growth, and relationships to women's issues, parenting, and social issues. Our mission is to publish quality books that will make a difference in people's lives—how we feel about ourselves and how we relate to one another. We value integrity, compassion, and receptivity, both in the books we publish and in the way we do business.

Our readers are our most important resource, and we value your input, suggestions, and ideas about what you would like to see published. Please feel free to contact us, to request our latest book catalog, or to be added to our mailing list.

Conari Press
An imprint of Red Wheel/Weiser, LLC
500 Third Sreet, Suite 230
San Francisco, CA 94107
www.redwheelweiser.com